CHIMPANZEES

by Jody Jensen Shaffer

ultant
n, PhD
oology
nesota

CORE
LIBRARY

Published by ABDO Publishing Company, PO Box 398166, Minneapolis, MN 55439. Copyright © 2014 by Abdo Consulting Group, Inc. International copyrights reserved in all countries. No part of this book may be reproduced in any form without written permission from the publisher. The Core Library™ is a trademark and logo of ABDO Publishing Company.

Printed in the United States of America,
North Mankato, Minnesota
092013
012014

♻ THIS BOOK CONTAINS AT LEAST 10% RECYCLED MATERIALS.

Editor: Mirella Miller
Series Designer: Becky Daum

Library of Congress Cataloging-in-Publication Data
Shaffer, Jody Jensen.
  Chimpanzees / by Jody Jensen Shaffer.
      pages cm. -- (The smartest animals)
  Includes bibliographical references and index.
  ISBN 978-1-62403-164-9
1. Chimpanzees--Juvenile literature. 2. Animal intelligence--Juvenile
literature. I. Title.
  QL737.P96S43 2014
  599.885--dc23
                          2013027267

Photo Credits: iStockphoto, cover, 1; J & C Sohns/Tier und Naturfotografie/SuperStock, 4; Marcl Schauer/Shutterstock Images, 7; Shutterstock Images, 9, 20; Fernando Sanchez Cortes/Shutterstock Images, 10; Sergey Uryadnikov/Shutterstock Images, 12, 45; Minden Pictures/SuperStock, 15; NHPA/SuperStock, 16, 22, 26 (bottom left), 36; Kristof Degreef/Shutterstock Images, 18, 43; Kitch Bain/Shutterstock Images, 25; Eric Isselee/Shutterstock Images, 26 (top left); Sharon Morris/Shutterstock Images, 26 (top right); Aaron Amat/Shutterstock Images, 26 (bottom right); Anup Shah/Thinkstock, 28; Red Line Editorial, 30; Sam D Cruz/Shutterstock Images, 32; Irina Afonskaya/Shutterstock Images, 34; National Geographic/Getty Images, 39

CONTENTS

CHAPTER ONE

GETTING TO KNOW OUR SUPER-SMART RELATIVES

In less time than it takes to blink, 11-year-old Ayumu can do something amazing. He is given less than half of one second to look at a computer screen with the numbers zero through nine randomly placed on it. Then he can correctly reorder them after they have been covered up. He is so fast, he outscores human adults twice his age! Ayumu's fastest record is

Chimpanzees are super-smart primates found in parts of Africa.

60 milliseconds. That is less than one second! Ayumu has been called a genius.

But Ayumu is no ordinary 11-year-old. He is a chimpanzee who outscored all humans who took the same memory test.

So Alike

Deoxyribonucleic acid (DNA) is a group of molecules inside cells. It contains a set of biological instructions that makes each species unique. Animals receive their DNA from their parents. Chimpanzee and human DNA are similar. Chimpanzees can even catch human diseases, such as the flu and the common cold. Biologically, chimpanzees are more closely related to humans than they are to gorillas.

Chimpanzee Basics

Chimpanzees are primates called apes. Apes share several traits. They do not have tails. Apes have broad chests and arms that can rotate easily. Apes are a group that includes gorillas, orangutans, and humans. Chimpanzees are one of humans' closest living relatives. Their genes are very similar to human

Male and female chimpanzees may develop white beards on their chins.

genes. And like humans, chimpanzees laugh, play, hug, and kiss.

Chimpanzees have black hair over most of their bodies. Hair does not grow on the palms of their hands, the soles of their feet, their ears, or their faces. They have big ears and flat noses. Some chimpanzees develop a white beard as they grow up.

Male chimpanzees are larger than females. A grown male stands approximately four feet tall (1.2 m). Males weigh between 86 pounds (39 kg) and 134 pounds (61 kg). Adult females are approximately three and a half feet tall (1 m). Females weigh between 69 pounds (31 kg) and 121 pounds (55 kg).

Captive chimpanzees are usually bigger than chimpanzees found in the wild.

Chimpanzees are quadrupeds. This means they move on all four limbs. Most of the time, chimpanzees walk on the knuckles of their hands and the soles of their feet. Their arms are longer than their legs. If they need to carry something, they can

Ape or Monkey?

People sometimes use the wrong word when describing monkeys and apes. But there are easy ways to tell which is which. Most monkeys have tails. They run along the tops of tree branches. Their arms and legs are nearly the same length. Baboons are monkeys. Chimpanzees are apes.
Apes do not have tails. They use their strong arms and shoulders to hang from tree limbs. They have longer arms than legs.

8

A chimpanzee's arms are longer than its legs. This means it can walk on all four limbs.

walk on just their feet. Each hand has four fingers and one opposable thumb. Opposable means the thumb can rest against the other fingers. Humans also have opposable thumbs. Chimpanzee feet have four toes and an opposable big toe. They use their opposable fingers and toes to grasp trees when they climb.

Chimpanzees enjoy grooming one another. Mothers help groom their babies.

A Day in the Life

The main social activity of chimpanzees is to groom one another. They push back the hair and inspect the skin. This act shows love or attention for another chimpanzee. Grooming also cleans the hair of lice, ticks, burrs, and dirt. The lice and ticks provide a snack for the groomer. Male chimpanzees are five times more likely to groom each other than females are to groom one another.

Chimpanzees spend six to eight hours a day looking for food and eating. They eat mostly fruits and leaves. But they also eat flowers, seeds, bark, and small animals, including insects and monkeys.

Each evening, chimpanzees build sleeping nests high in trees. Often built in the fork of two large branches, these nests are made by bending smaller branches together. A mother and her nursing baby share a nest. Chimpanzees usually do not sleep in the same nest twice.

EXPLORE ONLINE

The focus in Chapter One was on the characteristics of chimpanzees, including their intelligence. The Web site below gives more information about chimpanzee intelligence. As you know, every source is different. How is the information given on the Web site different from the information in this chapter? What information is the same? How do the two sources present information differently?

Chimpanzee Intelligence
www.mycorelibrary.com/chimpanzees

CHAPTER TWO

A CHIMPANZEE'S LIFE

A female chimpanzee is pregnant for more than seven months before giving birth. A baby chimpanzee weighs 3.7 pounds (1 kg) on average. Babies stay close to their mothers because they are too weak to move on their own. The mother cleans her newborn and encourages it to nurse. Baby chimpanzees have pink faces and a tuft of white hair on their bottoms.

Chimpanzee babies rely on their mothers during their first five or six years of life.

In the first few days, the mother will hold the baby with one arm while she uses her other three limbs to walk. Then baby chimpanzees hang on to the mother's stomach. At approximately six months, the infant begins riding on the mother's back. The infant watches its mother choose food, interact with other chimpanzees, make nests, and use tools. Chimpanzees learn by watching and by trying things themselves. The infant grasps food and feeds itself. It also takes its first steps.

For the next five or six years, the young chimpanzee plays with, learns from, and sleeps with its mother. The young chimpanzee also begins

Lost!

Like human children, young chimpanzees sometimes get lost. A chimpanzee may wander away from its mother while playing and only later realize it is alone. The baby may climb a tree to try and spot its mother. Or it may howl loudly and whine. Sometimes a mother chimpanzee will allow her youngster to wander away. Doing so teaches the baby independence. Most of the time, though, the mother is close by watching.

Baby chimpanzees hold onto their mothers' stomachs until they are about six months old.

to develop friendships apart from its mother. Young chimpanzees often play together. They jump, roll, spin, leap onto rocks, swing from branches, throw leaves, and even tease other animals, like baboons. Young males practice their charging displays. This is a way to show dominance by running, yelling, and throwing objects. Young males also begin to interact with older males.

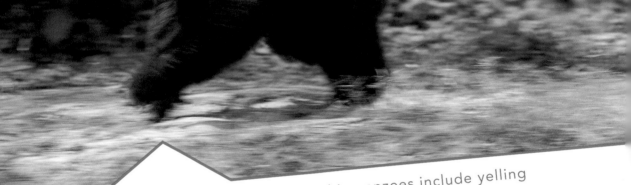

Charging displays by male chimpanzees include yelling and running around.

Mother chimpanzees are very patient with their offspring. If a mother sees her baby upsetting another member of the group, the mother guides the baby away. Father chimpanzees do not help care for their offspring. Male chimpanzees provide indirect care by protecting the group's home range from other chimpanzees.

Male chimpanzees that live in the wild are considered adults at approximately 15 or 16 years old. Female chimpanzees are considered adults around 13 years old. In captivity, chimpanzees grow and mature faster. Males and females would be considered adults around the age of 11 years old. In the wild, chimpanzees may live to be more than 50 years old. In captivity, few chimpanzees live to be more than 40 years old.

Mating

Female chimpanzees spend most of their time with their children and other females. When a female is between the ages of 12 and 15 years old, she usually leaves her mother's home range. She joins a neighboring chimpanzee community. This helps ensure that healthy offspring are produced. Mating within her original community could produce offspring who are too closely related.

Chimpanzees usually have one baby at a time, but they sometimes have twins. Females will not become

Female chimpanzees usually have one baby at a time. They care for this baby for about five years before having another baby.

pregnant again for five or six years after they give birth. Female chimpanzees mate with multiple males throughout their lives.

Social Organization

Chimpanzees live in loose groups called communities. Communities are made up of between 10 and 180 chimpanzees. Communities occupy a home range. A home range may be between 1.5 square miles and 33 square miles (4 sq km and 85 sq km) of land.

An alpha male leads each community. He can be young or old. The alpha is the highest ranking male in a community. Other males groom the alpha male and share food with him. But they may also challenge his leadership. Challenges include physical fights, charge displays, and

Border Patrol

Adult male chimpanzees periodically patrol the borders of their home range. They form a single line and silently leave their subgroup. This quiet behavior is different from their normal loud behavior. The patrollers are looking for members of other groups in their territory. If those on patrol outnumber the members of another group, they will launch an attack. Sometimes they hurt or kill the other group's chimpanzees.

Small chimpanzee parties travel and hunt together on the home range.

chasing the alpha. If another male successfully challenges the alpha, he will become the new leader.

Chimpanzees in a community usually do not travel together. The community forms into many different subgroups called parties. A party may have one chimpanzee traveling by himself. Or it may have dozens of chimpanzees gathered together.

Chimpanzees have very complicated social structures. In his book *Planet Ape*, Desmond Morris, a zoologist, relates how chimpanzees interact with one another:

> *The whole community may come together only rarely, such as at a particularly rich food source. Then they are off again, splitting up to rove in another series of subgroups, usually with around three to six members, keeping in contact with the rest of the community by loud calls. This fluid, dynamic social situation is known as the fission-fusion aspect of chimp society, and change can be rapid and without warning.*

Source: Desmond Morris and Steve Parker. Planet Ape.
Buffalo, NY: Firefly, 2009. Print. 186.

Consider Your Audience

Review this passage closely. How would you change it for a different audience, such as your parents or younger friends? Write a blog post explaining this same information to the new audience. How does your approach differ from the original text and why?

CHAPTER THREE

INTELLIGENT BEHAVIOR

One way scientists determine an animal's intelligence is by studying its ability to problem solve. Chimpanzees score well in this area. Scientists have discovered that chimpanzees behave and solve problems in ways they once thought only humans could.

Chimpanzees make and use tools. To reach termites in their nests, which look like large dirt

Chimpanzees solve problems by making and using tools.

Drink Up!

Dr. Michael Beran of Georgia State University researches chimpanzee intelligence. In one experiment, he wanted to see if chimpanzees could tell which of two cups had more liquid in it. Dr. Beran tested to see if the chimpanzees would pick the cup that was more full. Dr. Beran poured fruit juice into two cups as the chimpanzees watched. One cup was clear and the other was not. Dr. Beran repeated the test many times. During each test, he never poured the same amount of juice into the two cups. More than 75 percent of the time, the chimpanzees chose correctly! Even though the chimpanzees could not see how much juice was in the non-clear cup, they chose the cup with the most juice.

mounds, chimpanzees choose branches that will fit down termite holes. They strip leaves off the branches and poke them into the holes. Termites clamp onto the branches, and the chimpanzees eat the termites. Chimpanzees also use stones as hammers to break open hard-shelled nuts. They crumple leaves and use them as sponges to soak up water for drinking.

Chimpanzees use their intelligence to hunt. Chimpanzees eat

A chimpanzee's memory helps it remember what foods are in season or will make it feel better.

colobus monkeys after they have trapped them in the treetops.

Chimpanzees have great memories. They recall where certain fruit grows from season to season. They have even learned that eating special plants helps them feel better. Chimpanzees swallow leaves of the aspilia plant as if it were medicine to relieve stomach pain.

Chimpanzees appear to feel many emotions. These include joy, sadness, and fear. Chimpanzees

Chimpanzee Facial Expressions

Chimpanzees use their faces to help express themselves. A chimpanzee's smile, with top and bottom teeth showing, is an expression of fear. The excited, pant-hoot face is made by extending both lips and curving them at the ends. Chimpanzees that are playing cover their top teeth with their upper lips. A chimpanzee whose lips are together is interested. Why is it important for scientists to understand chimpanzee facial expressions?

also appear to experience jealousy. This happens when males are competing for a female.

Communication

Chimpanzees communicate with their voices and their bodies, just as humans do. They have a variety of calls.

These include grunts, screams, barks, whimpers, and pant-hoots. Pant-hoots are special calls that can be heard up to two miles (3.2 km) away. They are usually used when food has been found.

Chimpanzees also communicate nonverbally. They kiss, hug, give pats on the back, and hold hands. Some chimpanzees in captivity have learned many signs from American Sign Language (ASL). This is the language deaf humans use. Some chimpanzees can use more than 300 of these signs to communicate with scientists.

Chimpanzees and ASL

A female chimpanzee named Washoe was the first nonhuman to learn ASL. Washoe began learning ASL in 1966 and used approximately 250 different signs before her death in 2007. After moving to a chimpanzee sanctuary, Washoe began to teach another chimpanzee, Loulis, sign language without any human help. Washoe and Loulis communicated with each other in signs about how they were feeling.

CHAPTER FOUR

CHIMPANZEES UNDER THREAT

Chimpanzees live in Africa near the equator. Their range covers 900,000 square miles (2.3 million sq km). They live in tropical rain forests, swamp forests, and forest edges. They also live in open woodlands and dry savannahs.

Endangered and Threatened

Chimpanzees are endangered. This means there are very few chimpanzees left around the world. They

Chimpanzees live in many different habitats across Africa, including rain forests.

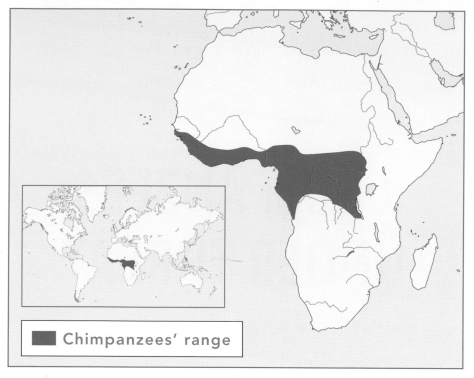

Chimpanzees' Range

This map shows the range of chimpanzees. As you can see, chimpanzees live in Africa. If you were a chimpanzee, why would you be well suited to this type of habitat? Use information from the chapter to back up your choice.

face many natural and human-made threats. Scientists estimate that in 1900, 2 million chimpanzees lived in the forests of Africa. Chimpanzee numbers have now fallen to between 150,000 and 300,000.

There are many threats to chimpanzees. Leopards and lions sometimes attack chimpanzees. But they are a small threat in comparison to humans. Humans hunt and bring diseases to chimpanzees. Humans cause habitat loss due to logging, development, and mining.

Logging destroys chimpanzee habitats. It may split up chimpanzee home ranges and populations. Clearing land for homes and farms also contributes to habitat loss. Villagers who live near chimpanzee habitats are often poor. They clear trees and land to plant crops to feed their families.

Mining gold, diamonds, graphite, and uranium also contributes to habitat loss. Soil is eroded during mining, and water is polluted.

Another threat to chimpanzees is their use for medical research.

Helping the Innocent

There are many organizations and people helping to protect chimpanzees and their homes. The Jane Goodall Institute, the Center for Great Apes, and the World Wildlife Federation are a few. Laws have been created that make it illegal to buy and sell wild animals, including chimpanzees. And tourists pay by the hour to see chimpanzees from a safe distance. That money helps care for chimpanzees and their habitats.

Activities like logging have ruined chimpanzees' home ranges.

Scientists use chimpanzees to try to find cures for human illnesses and diseases. Chimpanzees often get sick and die during this research. Medical research on chimpanzees is becoming less common. Some countries have banned this research.

Pet Chimpanzees

Sometimes baby chimpanzees are captured from the wild and sold as pets. Their mothers are almost always killed. When very young, baby chimpanzees are much like human infants. But as the chimpanzees become adults, they become big, dangerous, and hard to control. Owners usually lock them in cages for the rest of their lives.

Zoos and animal sanctuaries do not usually take former pet chimpanzees. They have not learned the social skills to live with other chimpanzees. Former chimpanzee pets usually end up in medical research.

Snared No More

In 2004, 5,000 chimpanzees lived in Budongo Forest in western Uganda. Twenty-five thousand people lived in villages and farms around the forest. They set snares to catch antelope and wild pigs. Chimpanzees sometimes got caught in the snares. They were often injured or killed. To help solve this problem, workers at Budongo Forest paid villagers to remove their traps. They also educated the people about the value of chimpanzees.

Some chimpanzees are put in cages and used for entertainment or medical research.

Baby chimpanzees captured for circuses, television, and movies have the same fate. They may have their teeth removed so they do not bite humans. They may be fitted with shock collars so they behave. These chimpanzees may also end up in medical research or be killed.

The Threat of Bushmeat

Chimpanzees face the threat of being killed for bushmeat. Bushmeat is meat from forest wildlife. Local people eat chimpanzees to survive. Some hunters are paid to kill chimpanzees. They send their meat across the world for people to eat. The bushmeat trade is estimated at $1 billion each year.

Disease and Illness

Illness and disease are also threats to chimpanzees. Tourists and researchers might leave behind diseases in chimpanzee home ranges. The chimpanzees can catch many of the illnesses humans suffer from. The common cold, tuberculosis, and the Ebola virus have killed many chimpanzees.

FURTHER EVIDENCE

There is quite a bit of information about the chimpanzee's range, habitat, and threats in Chapter Four. What do you think is the main point of the chapter? What evidence was given to support that point? Visit the Web site below to learn more about this topic. Choose a quote from the Web site that relates to this chapter. Does the quote support the author's main point? Does it make a new point? Write a few sentences explaining how the quote you found relates to this chapter.

Chimpanzee Range and Habitat
www.mycorelibrary.com/chimpanzees

CHAPTER FIVE

PAST, PRESENT, AND FUTURE

Much of what we know today about chimpanzees is from the work of Dr. Jane Goodall. Dr. Goodall first went to Africa in 1957 at age 22. At 26 years old, she traveled to Gombe Stream Game Reserve in Tanzania. She wanted to learn about chimpanzees.

Dr. Goodall discovered chimpanzees make and use tools. This exciting discovery helped scientists

Dr. Jane Goodall's research in Africa has provided information about chimpanzee life and behavior.

The Jane Goodall Institute

The Jane Goodall Institute was established in 1977 in the United States. It raises money for research at Gombe Stream Research Center. It also helps African villagers plant trees lost to logging. It educates people about conservation. The Jane Goodall Institute also cares for orphaned chimpanzees.

begin to understand how smart chimpanzees are. Dr. Goodall's work encouraged others to learn about chimpanzee intelligence.

Water as a Tool

At the Max Planck Institute for Evolutionary Anthropology in Leipzig, Germany, a researcher dropped a peanut down a long, clear tube that was attached to a female chimpanzee's cage. For ten minutes, the chimpanzee failed to figure out how to get the peanut out. Then suddenly, she gathered water in her mouth from her drinking bowl. She spit the water into the tube. This caused the peanut to float. She tried to grab the treat, but it was still too far away. She spit more water into the tube. This time

Different studies are done with chimpanzees to test their intelligence and problem-solving skills.

she could reach the peanut. This smart chimpanzee used water as a tool. Scientists use this test to better understand a chimpanzee's thought process when solving problems.

Working Together

Scientists know chimpanzees work well together. But they wondered if they would work together with humans. At the Great Ape Research Institute in Japan, scientists put this question to the test.

A male chimpanzee knew if he moved a stone, he could get the treat underneath. But when the stone was made heavier, he could not move it. Another chimpanzee appeared in the testing area. But the two did not work together to move the stone. Then a human appeared and tried to move the stone. The human was also unable to move the stone. Then the chimpanzee pulled with the human. They moved the stone. Later when the human was nearby but not helping, the chimpanzee walked to the human, grabbed her hand, and led her to the stone to help move it. This intelligent ape knows it needs help to get the treat.

Chimpanzee research continues to provide answers to scientists' questions about these super-smart animals. Chimpanzees are endangered and continue to be threatened by human activity. It is important for humans to help conserve chimpanzee habitats. That way these smart animals will be around for many more years.

In her book *Hope For Animals and Their World*, Dr. Goodall discusses how animal research helps humans understand similarities between themselves and animals. Here she points out the importance of chimpanzee research:

> *That study of chimpanzees, in Tanzania's Gombe National Park, has lasted for half a century and helped us understand, among other things, more about our own evolutionary history. . . .*
>
> *It has taught us that the similarities in biology and behavior between chimpanzees and humans are far greater than anyone had supposed. We are not, after all, the only beings with personalities, rational thought, and emotions. . .This understanding gives us new respect not only for chimpanzees, but also for all the other amazing animals with whom we share this planet.*

Source: Jane Goodall. "Excerpt: 'Hope for Animals and Their World' by Jane Goodall." ABC News. ABC News Network, September 4, 2009. Web. Accessed July 31, 2013.

What's the Big Idea?

Take a close look at Dr. Goodall's words. What is she trying to say about how humans perceive chimpanzees? Search this book to find evidence to support Dr. Goodall's research. Do you agree with Dr. Goodall?

Common Name: Chimpanzee

Scientific Name: *Pan troglodytes*

Average Size: Four feet (1.2 m) tall for adult males; three and a half feet (1 m) tall for adult females

Average Weight: 110 pounds (50 kg) for adult males; 85 pounds (38 kg) for adult females

Color: Mostly black

Lifespan: Up to 50 years in the wild

Diet: Chimpanzees eat mostly fruits and leaves. They also eat seeds, flowers, and small animals, including monkeys.

Habitat: Rain forests, woodlands, and savannahs of western and central Africa

Threats: Humans, leopards, and lions

Intelligence Features

- Chimpanzees make and use tools.
- Some chimpanzees have been taught and can use American Sign Language (ASL).
- Chimpanzees use a variety of vocal noises and body language to communicate.

STOP AND THINK

Dig Deeper

After reading this book, what questions do you still have about chimpanzees? Do you want to learn more about where chimpanzees live? Write down one or two questions that can guide you in doing research. With an adult's help, find some reliable sources about chimpanzees that can help answer your questions. Write a few sentences about what you learned from your research.

Take a Stand

This book discusses some of the problems encountered when chimpanzees and humans occupy the same areas. Take a position on limiting a chimpanzee's habitat. Then write a short essay explaining your opinion. Make sure you give reasons for your opinion. Give some evidence to support those reasons.

Say What?

Learning about chimpanzees can mean learning a lot of new vocabulary. Find five words in this book that you've never heard or seen before. Use a dictionary to find out what they mean. Using your own ideas, write down the meaning of each word. Then use each word in a new sentence.

Why Do I Care?

This book discusses how the chimpanzee population has declined greatly over the past 100 years. Even if you don't live near chimpanzees, why should you care about their decline? Write down two or three reasons humans should care about chimpanzee decline.

GLOSSARY

American Sign Language (ASL)
a system of hand gestures used to communicate

burrs
clinging seeds of plants

bushmeat
meat from wild animals

captivity
kept within bounds

charging display
when chimpanzees run, throw objects, and pant-hoot to show dominance

deoxyribonucleic acid (DNA)
substance that carries an organism's genes

endangered
a species that has become rare and is in danger of dying out completely

habitat
an animal's home environment, including plants and other animals

logging
cutting down trees for use in industry

primate
the group of mammals to which humans, monkeys, and apes belong

society
relationships and customs of a group

LEARN MORE

Books

Coxon, Michele. *Termites on a Stick: A Chimp Learns to Use a Tool*. New York: Star Bright Books, 2008.

Goodall, Jane. *The Chimpanzees I Love: Saving Their World and Ours*. New York: Scholastic Press, 2001.

Harris, Tim. *Chimpanzees*. Tucson, AZ: Brown Bear Books, 2012.

Web Links

To learn more about chimpanzees, visit ABDO Publishing Company online at **www.abdopublishing.com**. Web sites about chimpanzees are featured on our Book Links page. These links are routinely monitored and updated to provide the most current information available. Visit **www.mycorelibrary.com** for free additional tools for teachers and students.

INDEX

ABOUT THE AUTHOR

Jody Jensen Shaffer is a poet and the author of 14 books of fiction and nonfiction for children. She writes from the home she shares with her husband, two children, and dog in Missouri.